one hundred breaths

stephanie shields

First published in the United Kingdom 1st October 2018 by

one hundred breaths

Copyright © Stephanie Shields 2018

First Edition

ISBN 978-1-9164086-2-3

foreword

as humans, we're undeniably wired to tell stories—from whispered
bedtime tales to heartfelt recollections, from shared dreams to juicy
gossip. but i'm not so sure that us humans are equally wired to
write stories. for many of us (writers included), writing requires
herculean effort. motivation. self-bribery, even. that's why i consider
anyone who writes enough to make an actual book a badass who's
somehow managed to hack the business of being human.

all books are special, but this one particularly so. in 2015, i tried
something of an experiment and i called it only do one thing. i sent
out a daily email prompt that encouraged anyone who would listen
to do one simple life-enriching thing that day, that they might not
ordinarily do. one of those innocuous daily prompts was 'write a
100-word story'. i had no idea if anyone would take me up on my
challenge and override the fairly natural human propensity to shun
writing in favour of eating biscuits or watching re-runs of queer eye
or scrolling fruitlessly through social media. but someone out there
did. and she didn't stop there.

the result is this book of many stories. but it's also a book that tells
one story in particular: the story of what happens when you
challenge yourself to do something you wouldn't normally do. of
how only doing one thing differently can change everything.
without question, that's a story i want to read.

kate foster.

the little mask girl

eyes deceptively bright

red lips on a smile too wide

the little mask girl has it painted on for the world to see

a decoy from reality

hiding a heart like spun glass

skin as delicate as paper

too fragile to be handled without leaving a mark

but the scars left inside are the worst of all

searing wounds across the heart and soul

hidden too deep to share

and sometimes the mask slips, the paper tears, the spun glass shatters

no sellotape, no glue, can repair the damage or fix the mess

maybe you've seen her

maybe she's you

why not be you?

this year, why not be you?

why not be who you are in your secret heart, why not shine your light to the world and shut the door on those that dim your soul.

go out with your colours blazing. shake the tree branches. rattle the windows. shout from the hills and dance down the lanes.

nail your colours to the mast, wear your heart on your sleeve, and paint a sign on your chest saying "i love being me and i'm not going to change any more"

this year say i am here and i am never going away.

she listened

she listened when they said that children are seen and not heard

she listened when they insisted it wasn't appropriate for girls

she listened when they interrupted her

she listened when they talked over her

she listened when they told her to be quiet

she listened when they said she didn't know what she was talking about

she listened when they told to her not to speak

she listened when they said to shut up

she listened to everything telling her not to make a noise until one day she opened her mouth and no sound came out at all.

chasing new horizons

the horizon was silver and red and gold and he wanted it. he always wanted it.

he didn't see the beauty of the greens and blues around him as he went towards. he didn't understand how to appreciate what was already there.

the earth span as he ran, tipping the colours, rendering him always chasing, always in pursuit.

until one day he stopped and looked around. as he did, the familiarity of the greens and blues settled on him.

because the earth is round and if you run for long enough you will always end up back where you started.

fishing for wishes

as the earth dreams she casts her net for wishes, the hidden hopes
and desires of the human soul hooked as they sleep.

glittering, glistening, translucent, each wish pulsing with the beat of
a human heart, and just as fragile.

she tends to them, whispering, coaxing, encouraging; filling them
with the ability to be fulfilled. then lets her net fall, wishes tumbling
back to earth, each renewed with hope and potential.

for is it not said,

"grant someone a wish and you satisfy them for a day; help them to
grant their own wishes and you satisfy them for life."

the artist

outside it was a wasteland, desolate. nothing living, nothing growing, nothing thriving. left undeveloped, unused, unloved.

she looked at the space and imagined how to fill it. who would live there? who could love it?

green spaces and tall trees. the sound of dogs barking and children playing.

she sketched as she imagined, her pencil chalking outlines of a world captured static on a page.

as night fell she drifted to sleep, dreaming of what could be.

what could be.

the next day the pages of her sketchbook were blank but outside she could hear the sound of children playing.

the cloud elves

the cloud elves see everything. the cloud elves collect everything. the cloud elves share everything.

they make pictures appear all over the world. they bring music to hospital beds. they share stories to delight small children.

they spread the laughter and also the tears. they can make it sunrise at bedtime and provide snowfall in july.

any tale, any picture, any moment; they save it, curate it, keep it forever.

the cloud elves see everything. the cloud elves collect everything. the cloud elves share everything. maybe, if you look up at just the right time, you might see them too.

the star and the sun

the star shone with all its might, casting silvery light across the sky

slowly, lazily, the sun rose, bright yellow beams stretching across the earth.

the star slipped away unnoticed, dwindling, diminished into insignificance by the majesty of the sun.

the sun was smug, taking this disappearance as right and proper tribute to its own brilliance.

but the earth moved and the day passed and slowly the sun began to slip and fade, yellow to burnished orange, tinged red then pink and fading.

and slowly the star began to shine, content to take its place in the sky once more.

the sea beyond

when will we reach the sea?

is it round the next corner?

or the next?

the soft sigh of a wave, the slight smack of saltiness in the air. an evocative glimpse of blue, shimmering, then gone with the bend in the road.

when will we reach the sea?

is it round the next corner?

or the next?

the plaintive cry of the gulls growing stronger, wheeling and diving in the sky. the noise of crashing waves building, that elusive promise of what lies beyond.

when will we reach the sea?

is it round the next corner?

or the next?

lady, will you walk with your friend?

lady, will you walk with your friend?

the path now dappled with sunlight will also be dark at times. it will twist and turn. there are ravines so deep they cannot be measured and inclines so high they cannot be imagined. there are the widest most open of roads and also the narrowest of tightropes over unfathomable depths. the light may blind you or the darkness be so strong you cannot know where to put your feet.

but even when it's so black you cannot see i promise i will always be here.

lady, will you walk with your friend?

guarding.

the door was solid. locked. impregnable. a fearsome barrier against the outside world.

guards stood by it day and night. stoic. impassive.

there were no signs to say what was inside, nothing to show what their duty protected.

no-one in living memory had ever seen the door opened, nor had even the most skilled of cat burglars ever made it inside.

"a fortune," the people said. "the most precious of jewels to be kept safe always."

but what if the guards weren't protecting what was behind the door?

what if they were protecting the public from it ever getting out.

the audience.

he plays a note and the audience turn. he plays another and they go still, conversations falling away, drinks forgotten.

the notes ripple and twist through the air, hanging high, ebbing, falling, fading.

the audience are captivated, spellbound. nothing exists in that moment except watching; listening; feeling the swell of the music.

the notes dance around them, filling them, transporting them. each evoking different feelings, memories, desires. taking them to a different time and a different place; a different version of themselves.

he plays the last note then…silence. the song is finished and the audience are released from the spell.

the demon who lived in a well

a many-headed multi-tentacled demon, with claws instead of
suckers, lived at the bottom of a well.

unsurprisingly, it wasn't very happy about this.

it was dark and wet and when people used the well the bucket
would drop and always hit one of its heads.

but people also used the well for wishes, throwing in gold and
silver coins as they wished.

one day, after another bucket / head interface, the demon counted
up the coins. it was a fortune.

the demon now lives in the côte d'azur, drawing beautiful sunsets.
it hasn't been hit by a bucket in years.

good fences make good neighbours

they lived as neighbours and friends for years.

but one man worried for his lands and he built a wall to defend them.

his neighbour asked, "why did you do that?"

"to defend myself and my lands," he replied.

so his neighbour built a bigger wall.

"why did you do that?"

"i need to defend myself and my lands too," the neighbour replied.

so the first man made his wall higher. then his neighbour made his higher still.

their walls became so high they could no longer see each other and they forget their neighbour had ever been their friend.

the path

the world was grey. always grey. but she wanted more.

everyone said that was dangerous, to stick to well known places and well used paths. but she was never very good at listening.

she saw a path strewn with brambles and pebbles underfoot. nothing to indicate it was known or safe. so she stepped on it.

and discovered above the grey, there was sun and warmth. green grass and blue sky. and she marvelled that a world so full of grey below should contain such beauty above.

just because no-one else has taken that path doesn't that mean you shouldn't.

a picture

they say a picture paints a thousand words. whoever they may be. how do they know?

a picture can be an impression, an interpretation. a gift, a memory of a great night out.

framed, hung, centred. well lit and prominent.

or is it a reminder of a time best forgotten? seedy, dirty, a relic of days preferred lost to the past. locked away in an attic, gathering dust and wrinkles.

flattery or sycophancy? art or abomination?

bawdy and licentious; coy and demure; angular and incomprehensible.

if a picture paints a thousand words, then what does your picture say about you?

the wave that wanted to be first

the wave wanted to be the first, to be the fastest; the most fastest wave that there ever was.

it crashed through the sea, white-topped, racing its way to the shore, hungry for the glory, the win.

"i want to be first, i want to be first, i want to be first" it thought eagerly as it crested over all the other waves, faster and faster.

it didn't care about enjoying the journey, it just wanted to hit the destination quickest.

"made it!" it thought ecstatically as it crashed onto the beach then slowly seeped into the sand without trace.

antihope

hope is a thing with feathers
singing blithely away
with wings that can lift us beyond all expectation
helping our souls to fly

> hope can live on the smallest of morsels
> a smile, a sunbeam
> an incorrect diagnosis

> hope keeps us warm when reason has fled
> hope gives us the courage to get out of bed
> hope helps us think maybe
> hope offers a chance

hope can tangle our emotions in a complicated dance
but sometimes there is nothing to feed hope except hope itself
and that becomes lies

> and so, like all things with feathers,

> one day hope dies.

the trees

the trees in the parks grew tall and straight and green.

people sat under them, appreciating the leafy shade they provided from the hot sun as they ate their lunches and read their books and their newspapers

but there wasn't enough paper to keep getting all of these things printed. "we must have our news", the people said, "we must have our books and our magazines."

so the trees were cut down and pulped and there were no leafy green spaces at lunchtime anymore.

and the people wrote letters to the newspapers to complain about the trees being cut down.

pandora

the town was full of forethought. no-one ate to excess. relationships were chaste. nobody ever wanted more than their share.

work was done rarely, as the people couldn't be bothered. what was done was done sloppily, as they didn't take pride in their achievements. yet no-one was cross about the bad workmanship as it never occurred to them to shout.

competition was unheard of. who wanted more money? why did it matter if others had something you had not?

yet slowly the people stagnated.

and there was no hope of it ever changing because pandora had never opened the box.

meetings

nothing was getting done and nobody knew why and so they put it on the agenda for their next meeting.

they held pre-meeting meetings and post-meeting meetings and meetings about the meetings to come..

and still nothing was getting done. so they scheduled another meeting to look into why they were so busy.

"but what if we stopped having meetings" said a small voice. "maybe then we wouldn't be so busy?"

so they formed a committee and set up an enquiry, all to look into the meetings. and this generated more meetings than ever before.

and still nothing was done.

the sky over our heads

the shifting clouds overhead. wide open ever-changing skies.

how can we ever understand the vastness of our world if we don't open our eyes?

we can't. it's too big, immense, immeasurable. we can't control it. we can't comprehend it. we can merely observe it in passing.

streaks of pink purple, red yellow. blazen and unstoppable. majestic. then the bluest of midnights, laced with a thousand tiny stars.

over your head and over mine.

we never know what is coming, what each new day will bring. until one day, nothing comes at all.

but until that time, underneath it we dance.

a dog and his ball

i watched the dog nudging the blue ball along the pavement, tail wagging as he followed it.

nothing else seemed to exist for him but this blue ball.

i waited for him to pick it up, to take it over to his owner to play. and he didn't. he just kept nudging and following it. and then i saw the green ball already in his mouth.

you can't pick up a new ball when you're carrying the old one.

sometimes you have to play with your own ball and let the one on the ground roll away to someone else.

birthdays

birthdays

special days

starred on the calendar days

of cake and candles

of gifts and cards

of gleeful anticipation

and crushing disappointment

the fixed smile of gratitude

the flurry of "oh you shouldn't haves"

the secret hope for that one perfect gift

lost in the beguiling allure of a scarlet red ribbon

jelly and ice-cream

postal vouchers

book tokens

remembering birthdays past

and celebrating with those no longer here

the shimmering heat haze from the candles

wondering 'how did it get to be so many?' eyes closed,

blowing them out,

fervently thinking "i wish…"

another year older

another year.

another

dawn

they will be coming soon.

i do not know how to write all there is in my heart.

dawn comes soon, bringing the light, and so they come, to take away all the light in my world.

things could not have been done differently yet i never expected it would be those closest to me making this happen.

my dearest love, there are no words but you are not here and so i am reduced to words. to tell you i love, to tell you i will always love you.

dawn comes and so do they.

goodbye, my love.

goodbye.

pain

it hits you, hard and unexpected.

it is all-consuming. like there has never been anything in the world but it. you can't ever imagine a time it wasn't there.

it claws at you, a monster ripping you open from the inside.

all you can do is control your breathing. in. and out. just to get through to the next second. and then the next.

nails in your palms, creating more hurt to distract from the real hurt.

wave upon wave of pain.

then one day it's gone. and it's like you can't ever imagine a time when it was there.

conquering the fear

you have to own it.

go on, admit that thing you want more than anything else.

now work on it. craft it. make it yours.

ask for help. draw on the experiences of others.

maybe you will fail. maybe you will fail a thousand times. maybe you will go down in a blaze of glory and always be known for it.

but maybe, just maybe, you will succeed. you will breathe fire over your naysayers and celebrate your triumph with your friends. yours is a name for the history books.

but first you have to own it.

just own it.

please don't turn out the light

please don't turn out the light.
it's dark.
i'm scared.

> where am i?
> what is this place?

i don't like it.
i can't see you.
please don't turn out the light.

> did i say something?
> did i not do something?
> i don't want to be here.

please don't turn out the light.

> i don't know what's happening.
> it's hard to breathe.
> it's hard not to cry.

please don't turn out the light.
i'm very frightened now.
i really don't want to be here.
this isn't funny anymore.

> will you come back?
> i need you.

please don't turn out the light.

rat race

bed

the insomnia the alarm the shower the coffee the commute

a hastily scanned timeline a facebook status update

meeting upon meeting upon meeting upon meeting

email report email writing email

damn it email will you all email just stop email it email with email all the email emails

lunch a salad snatched at your desk

the mid afternoon slump

biscuits

pub drinks only staying for one leaving five later

kebab

the night bus

bed

insomnia the alarm the shower the coffee the commute

a hastily scanned timeline a status update

sometimes

don't you wish

it would all just

stop

reaching for the stars

the stars twinkled high in the sky. the occasional darting light of a comet, streaking briefly for fame.

the little girl gazed up and up; wanting to live in the sky, wanting to be a star.

but everyone told her to keep her feet on the ground. "stars aren't for the likes of us."

still she kept on looking and hoping and wishing. a star was the only the thing that would truly satisfy her.

until one day she hooked her little finger round the corner of a star. she floated up into the sky and was never seen again.

if you were my lover

if you were here…

…i'd wind you in my arms, as titania to bottom

…i'd grant you a thousand kisses, such as catullus

…i'd be wide eyed that you kiss by the book, as juliet to romeo

if you were my lover…

…i'd light that green light in the bay, as daisy did for gatsby

…i'd make you know the meaning of tomorrow, as scarlet to rhett

…you'd wear my pearls, as cheri wore colette's

if you were mine…

then alike as benedick to beatrice… i would love nothing in the world as well as you. is that not strange?

book on a shelf

a book waved to me from the shelf

let's go on an adventure, it seemed to say

we'll hijack a hot air balloon and go where the wind blows us.

over the seas, high above the pirates

into the mountains with dragons and down into the dells with the dwarves

we can camp out under the stars and see what strange creatures visit our fire

"not today, book" i had to say. "it is my lunch hour and i must return to work"

but all afternoon i carried that adventure in my heart.

and my boss accused me of daydreaming.

the destruction of art

deep slashes across the mona lisa's enigmatic smile

a bomb under the pyramids, reducing them to rubble

your words spit out, hot and angry and hurtful

searing across our love like a brand

the bayeux tapestry is now unstitched

that needle scratched across beethoven's fifth

terrible things never to be unsaid

our relationship teeters on the edge of the abyss

graffiti daubed on rodin's kiss

the sistine chapel painted over

the louvre looted

and every mirror in the hall of versailles smashed

the deliberate destruction of great works of art

and that's now what your silence does to my heart

holes in the fabric of night

a little girl gazed at the stars and thought they were holes cut in to the fabric of night and wondered what there was on the other side.

"they are rocks, little girl, only rocks," the grown ups said.

she didn't believe them, no matter how often they said it or how many science books they showed her.

but she did learn enough science to build a rocket so she could see for herself.

and so up she flew into the sky and straight through one of the holes in the night to see the world on the other side.

the travelling egg

a travelling egg

rolled to the circus

to see what he could be.

he painted his face

to joke with the clowns

but he avoided the lions

too scary

he wobbled his way

along a high-wire

and established himself

as a deadset high flier

but then came the day

that fate had a say

oh travelling egg

oh travelling egg

you wouldn't listen

when they all said...

an egg in a cannon?

that's just not going to happen

but happen it did

and fired you were

up into sky

flying so high

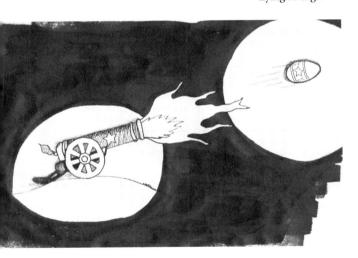

then landing

splat

and so that was that.

maybe

maybe they should never have met

maybe their paths should never have crossed

maybe they shouldn't have shared so much so deeply

maybe they should never have kissed

maybe he should have said something

maybe she should have walked away

maybe it was everything

maybe it was nothing

maybe it was all it could ever be right then

maybe it was a love to sear the soul

maybe it wasn't

maybe it was sweet

maybe it shouldn't have hurt so much

maybe it was never real

maybe he just liked the version of himself he saw reflected in her eyes.

monday night

it's monday night. i walk into the store as a woman drops part of her shopping, a bottle of perrier smashing at my feet.

i get my wine & jump the queue as no-one else wants to use the self-service till.

a staff member authorises me as being over 25.

i pay cash & one coin keeps being rejected.

the same staff member cancels the sale.

i try again.

the same coin gets rejected.

he goes to the till & swaps it for a new one.

the sale goes through.

all the while spilt perrier seeps across the supermarket floor.

brighter in the dawn

in the depths of midnight all seems hopeless.

dreams are lost in the unscaleable dark; hopes fall into the abyss of night. the three o'clock in the morning voice whispers hopelessness

then as the first slivers of dawn pierce the sky, the sun begins the majestic rise to banish night and doubt.

the sounds of awake; the stillness, the pump of hot water, the distant siren and clatter of the milkfloat, all add up to banish the night terrors.

the clock ticks inexorably towards the day

hope returns undaunted

and with it the knowledge that this too can be done.

5 am

i woke suddenly in the dark

disorientated

where was i?

what was this place?

then slowly reality took shape

and i could hear you breathing

the soft almost silent noise of someone who has been told all their
life not to make a sound

so i lay there and i listened and i luxuriated

you

asleep

peaceful

and happy, i hoped

i could feel your warm skin against mine

the salt sweat taste still present on my lips

i willed the police helicopter into silence

wanting you to sleep for longer

then your alarm went off

and we both swore

bruise

there is a bruise on my left breast

i look at it, surprised

trying to remember how

in the tangle of limbs and lust

of wine and words and whispered promises

this damage occurred

you weren't always gentle

i didn't always mind

it was carnal. and curious

mutually gloriously selfishly sexual

but i hadn't truly estimated the damage.

i touch the bruise, tentatively

remembering.

i haven't noticed the tears that begin silently falling

a bruise on my left breast

rising and falling as my heart beats

touching the bruise was nothing compared to the pain of never
seeing you again.

breathing

i love you, he said

                i love you too, she said, i think

the silence stretched out between them

when it comes to love, who can know the shape or form or truth of
it

             i don't understand love, she said eventually

   how do you know how to love? how do you know it is love? how
                            can you be sure?

he laughed and gathered her in his arms

i've never worked out how breathing works, he replied, but i seem
to manage that just fine.

and they sat and they breathed and they loved and everything was
just fine.

draft

please forgive me

i wasn't intended to be written this way

i have been launched, unedited,

into a world that demands perfection

i am unformed, unfinished

i am rough about my edges

the idea is good

but the execution lacks skill, lacks grace

i cannot express what i desire, what i want

my shapings do not give me this ability

i blunder crudely through life,

my flaws exposed

a lack of attention to detail

has made me what i am

so please forgive the strange, the angular, the blurted words, the perpendicular

i wasn't intended to be written this way

signposts

the signpost made it sound intriguing

the pathway looked smooth

the views were pretty spectacular.

of course you wanted to go there.

but slowly that signpost faded

the path got rougher, harder to climb

and there seemed to be too many things blocking the view

which, let's face it, wasn't looking all that great anymore

you can admit you no longer want to go there

you may turn around

you are allowed to stop

walk away from this place

kick that dust off your feet

there are other signposts

other paths

other views

which way do you want to go?

the risks of taking the world by storm

do you want to take the world by storm, my son?

to tell of love and truth and the strumming of mandolins

the tumultuous applause, the shining spotlight

the breathless hush

be bold

your symphony is epic

play it loud and unapologetic

yet be prepared, for the final chord

for the loss and endings and the playing of the worlds' smallest violins

the clapping ends, the audience file out

this particular show is over.

their gratitude is unsaid

their silence unsympathetic

yet you're not heartbroken,

you've just discovered that the world no longer beats to the sound of your drum

hearts desire

let me take you on a journey of your own imagination

let us stroll together through the palace of your dreams

this night you can have

your secret wish

your most heartfelt desire

no need to be hasty in your choosing

we have all night to trip through your wantings

let us tarry by the pinnacle of your wishings

let us circle the summit of your desire

such longings should not be satisfied willy-nilly

think carefully on what you believe you desire

for tonight you will get all you ever dreamed of

you can remember some of your dreams, right?

the dance

"let's dance," she said.

"i don't dance," he said.

"such a shame," she said.

"would you not like to do this?"

she span and her wings spread,

shining, glittering, mesmerising.

"i would like to," he said.

"but that is not dancing."

she paused and considered, her head on one side, studying him as a cat might study a mouse.

"is it not? you know this? you, who does not dance?"

she approached, slowly, determinedly, and there was nowhere for him to go.

her wings spread around him, trapping him, lifting him, spinning him.

"let me show you how to dance."

i just fucking miss you

i miss you. i just fucking miss you, ok?

who is this about? who fucking knows?

i know. i know how all the jagged pieces of my broken heart have fallen

i know the loss of you and you and you

i know that i can't say this. i know you do not have the ears to hear it not the emotional capacity to comprehend it

yet i have such depths to feel it.

i could scream it, cry it, sigh it, lie about it.

but i feel it. i feel it every day.

i just fucking miss you, ok?

gardens

you tend your bad feelings as a gardener tends a garden

keeping every pleasure pruned away

the thorns on the rose bushes left sharply pointed, no flowers bloom here

let not the unwary stray into your feelings

for fear they be pricked on your displeasure

no happiness is allowed to shine

enjoyment is uprooted like a weed

and at the end of the day do you sit in the deckchair of your imagination?

to look out at your sourness and think what fine work you have done?

and block out the sounds of love and laughter from the gardens nearby?

you

you are as familiar to me as as my home in the dark

i know my way around without need of lights or candles

all your curves, all your angles. all the hard planes that make you
you

i can find the comfiest places and curl up without hesitation,
knowing where is warm and where is safe

but sometimes, like an unknown moved piece of furniture, i
encounter a part of you i didn't know was there. sharp and painful
and unexpected.

and, like with a stubbed toe in the dark, i am left bruised and
reaching for the light-switch

fuck sensible

fuck sensible

fuck saving for a rainy day

fuck carrying an umbrella "in case it rains"

fuck waiting

fuck queuing

fuck believing in a happy ending instead of making it happen

fuck "maybe"

fuck "one day"

fuck beige

fuck "keeping for best"

fuck keeping your head when all about you are losing theirs

fuck not blowing your own trumpet

fuck calling cake "naughty" or eating salad being "good"

fuck ordinary

fuck extraordinary

fuck good intentions

fuck keeping calm and carrying on

fuck scared

fuck never being for the rest of your life the person you want to be

fuck this

how to assume power

release wild beasts into the street

see the people panic and shriek

then calmly send out your guard

announce that you are taking charge

issue an order then another

remind them not to hurt each other

whilst quietly pointing out the flaws

of the people not like yours

assume power, ascend the throne

turn your back on those who moan

now's the time, why even wait

to rule your own created state

but don't dismiss the talk as blather

from those that stop to gather

for how will you know what to do

when someone releases wild beasts on you

one

you wash up

sometimes

a bowl, a plate, a knife, a fork,

the occasional saucepan

and a variety of teaspoons

the grater gets a star turn

yet increasingly less so

after all, pre grated cheese is a thing

and if not for you then who?

you persist with the grater

and resist pre sliced onions and mushrooms for all that they could
imply

yet it remains one glass

one mug

the very crockery of loneliness

as the candles flicker and the clock ticks on

and sometimes, sometimes, the only reason to go to bed is because
the bottle is empty.

champagne in the bath

i drink champagne

in the bath

alone

and i think of you

you

you

your touch

your voice

your everything

i think of your lips

how they curve

how they feel

as the cold bubbles burst on mine

the angry planes of your body

the demanding nature of your touch

so strong

so unyielding

so much

and yet

and yet

you are so soft

so lost

and i have found you

even though you never wanted to be found

the bath cools

the bottle empties

and i am left

cold

alone

yet there are other baths

other bottles

other you.

maybe hell does exist

maybe hell does exist

maybe it's the reminders of our failures

maybe it's the disappointment on the faces of others

those times when we could've tried but didn't

it's every friend we let down with a lie

it's every homeless person we walk on by

it's the sight of ourselves when we aren't honest

or true to beliefs

those images, streaming endlessly past our eyes

forced to remember we weren't what we hoped to be

wanted to be

thought we were

maybe

maybe

if hell does exist, whilst we are still alive we could be a bit more
right now

hiding from the world

you keep your head down as you walk

avoiding eye contact with passers-by

at work your smile is a bland mask

inscrutable

at home you don't draw back the curtains

allowing no natural light

you don't want to let the world see you

you don't want to be distracted from the beauty that is out there

you don't want to feel

to be reminded of feeling

but those people that you walk past

those ones you shut out and ignore

do you never realise that they are hurting too

and that one smile from you would light up their world

stumble. jumble. crumble.

i daren't tell you how i feel

my fingers stumble over the keyboard

my mouth can't shape the words.

i breathe out just a little

as i fumble my way through

this thing we call a life

yet i remain motionless, paralysed by indecision

as my thoughts tumble around me

like leaves strewn in the autumn wind

i know i have to act

this jumble of emotions inside me

cannot be ignored, cannot be neglected

but to act and be rejected cannot be considered

i would falter, crumble, fall

better sometimes not to act and to say nothing at all.

london dust

you get home for the evening
you kick off your shoes and you wash your hands
cleansing away the dust of the day

but this is london dust.
swept from the tortured stones of the tower
carried on merchant ships down river
spun on the eye
threaded through cleopatra's needle
blown on the breeze to nelson, lofty with his pigeons
then shaken with the toll of big ben

this is the dust of ages
carrying the capital and its history
into a shiny and uncertain future
where monuments are still to be built
based on stories yet to be told

there are only two sounds in my flat

there are only two sounds in my flat

the first is the ticking of clocks

slightly out of time

one hand offsetting the other

they count down the inevitable hours, minutes, seconds. each as

measured, as long, as short, as the last

the second sound is my breathing

slow

steady

the compression and expansion of my lungs

the breath, inhaling

exhaling

oxygen. nitrogen. hydrogen.

all inter-mingled.

this, too, marks the passing of time

the inexorable move in to the future

time passes.

breathing passing.

there are only two sounds in my flat

one day there will only be one sound.

please go away

your every message

your every smile

and every time you post an oh so subtle online denial

those facebook pokes

your subtle in-jokes

and each time something inside me chokes

i do not envy you your joy

your rapture

it just makes me want to hasten to the hereafter

your love is joyous

freeing

all consuming

but for me

only loneliness is looming

it's not that i want you

far from that

it's that i want the same

for me

my 'that'

so do not pity me when i say

i am happy for you

and now please go away

what is truth?

what is truth, asked jesting pilate

in this time of #fakenews, political spin, this denigration of democratic values

all for the headline, the soundbite, the win

to spread fear, to pursue power

how to know

when the media lie in bed with the rulemakers

the new truthmakers

what is truth

what is fact

what is real

time perhaps to listen

not to words but the stories unsaid

and those that emerge

on days good to bury bad news

then, with our facts, with our power

it is time to stand and declaim

this is my truth, now tell me yours

water

the water flows swiftly under the bridge

a siren's call of adventure

to something better

something new

and you wonder if you followed, if you went with it

where could it take you

what mysteries could you see

day after day

watching

imagining

an irresistible urge to be swept away

and you step and you step

the cold shock of it numbing

and you step and you step

your footing stumbling

and as you feel the water closing over you realise

that it is taking you to place from which you can never return

and any postcards are always undelivered

blossom

a snowdrop

a daffodil

a crocus

those gloriously coloured

harbingers of spring

and also blossom

blossom

everywhere

on branches, in the air, falling

blown from the boughs

and strewn down the street as though in a 'first confetti to reach the finish line' race

those delicate petals making a bridal path for those who will never walk that aisle

yet in creating such a beautiful carpet it has already hastened its decay

to be trodden underfoot and swept into the gutter

forgotten

until next spring

for it will come back

it won't be this blossom

but it will be blossom

crumbs of comfort

do not settle for less than you deserve

every mouthful

every morsel

every piece

is yours

you do not have to beg for scraps from someone else's table

your life is bountiful

plentiful

do not let someone else choose

how often you get fed

and what you eat

you do not need permission for your appetite

no-one else gets to select or edit your menu

life should make you hungry

and your hunger should be satisfied

do not settle for less than you deserve

for a careless smile or an occasional thought

crumbs of comfort do not make a loaf.

we are writers

write boldly or not at all

no other words are yours

can be yours

this is your story

your time

not for you the anodyne

the banal

the bland

you are not made to use the words of others, to hide behind them

delve into your world of horror and terror and glamour and
romance

draw your audience in with the most human of acts and the
supreme intervention of gods

no tale is too tall

no encounter too small

write to encompass the entirety of the universe and every hidden
piece

we are writers, my friends

we are writers

magic

they gave all they had to the fairies, wanting their son to be blessed with good looks, wealth, and a long life.

and as he grew up everyone loved him

but his friends grew older. his parents grew older still

and his handsome face developed no line or wrinkle

nor did the coins in his coffers dwindle

it came to pass his parents died

and his friends did too

and he remained, with his looks, wealth, and long long life

why?, he asked. why?

your parents asked for magic, the fairies replied. they never asked for it to be good.

comfort zones

why do you stay?

you do not need to be here

these walls are of your own making

of your own fear

you may perceive it to be safe

but how would you know what the risks are?

when did you last step outside

outside that door

outside your comfort zone

when were you last challenged

shaken

moved

when did you last decide to take a step off the specified path?

we can all be any one we want to be inside our own heads

but who are you to everybody else?

and more, who do you want to be?

existence

i don't know how to explain it
i don't know how to explain you
to me

　　　　　　　you exist

　　　　　　　　　　　　i exist

we hold these truths to be self evident
and yet, and yet
we met and it was like you had always been there
i have scoured my memory
no-one has imprinted themselves on my soul before

　　　　　　　like this

　　　　　　　　　　　like you

i played it cool, of course
bought another drink
but for me there was no other place in the world
for you
for me

　　　　　　　for here

　　　　　　　　　　　for us?

but by the time i said so, you had found somebody else.

watching

so i'm sitting on my patio and it's nearly midnight

and i'm watching cars roll up and down the street

and i'm like do you not need to go home

a light across the road shows the park patrol,

patrolling

a taxi stops, spilling out two girls, women

drunk, beautiful, happy

and now it's gone midnight

and i'm watching cars still roll up and down the street

and i'm like do you not need to go home at all

all the park gates are closed now

and i should go to bed

yet i'm still sitting on my patio

watching

heart soar

you make my heart soar

it leaps in my chest

beating wildly

it greets you before i even know you are there

time passes

the pace slows

my pulse drops

and the realisation slowly creeps

that there is no corresponding beat

that leaps to meet with mine

my heart retreats

wounded

your heart beats on

seemingly unaffected

days pass

weeks pass

months

my heart heals

slowly

and then one day there you are

you say hello

and my heart leaps in my chest

beating wildly

greeting you before i even knew you were there

again

you make my heart sore

reflections

she checked her outfit anxiously

smoothed the material, twisted this way and that

please make me look good

her reflection was eager to please

but she couldn't see it

> he looked in the mirror, tried to fix his hair
>
> told himself he looked great
>
> his reflection agreed enthusiastically
>
> but his heart wasn't in it
>
> his fear was he was inadequate

and this pattern repeated in mirrors all over the world, night after night

> and so the people slept, unhappy and unfulfilled

and yet while they slept, their reflections, sleeker, happier, infinitely more confident, slipped away to parties of their own

under the eaves

under the eaves the birds peep
their wings rustle
maybe today is the day
maybe

they jostle for position
some fighting to be first
some hoping to be last
the chirrups and the cheeps
like rowdy teenagers
full of swagger and bravado
and look at me cool
yet that hesitant look over the shoulder before they leap
and launch themselves into a world
where they are untested, unknown

and you look round at your hallway suddenly unfilled with
discarded trainers
and the fridge with no empty milk bottles returned
as you listen under the eaves
to where the birds peep

phoebe

gazing into the sky at night

it is to phoebe i look

pillowed on her clouded bed

pale, beautiful, waxing, waning

and to her i say

you traitorous bitch

my love wrote poetry for you and you watched him as he fucked her against that wall

what price those love poems now?

what joy is there in that adoration of your majesty, your pale pearlescence, when dark-eyed milk-skinned beauties are so readily to hand?

i was jealous of his love for you. he never wrote poetry for me, you see

but then he never fucked me against a wall either.

all the words have been written

all the words have been written
there are no more words

let the speakers fall silent
let the authors set down their pens
all that is written has been spoken
this is where the story ends

may the politicians cease their rhetoric
may the journalists no longer report on the news
the time of the headline is over
and all of the wordsmiths are gone

put aside your dictionaries
dwell no more on crossword clues

turn off that light in the library
and lock the door for evermore

all the words have been written
now there are no more words

daydreaming

the alarm is already on snooze

as she hides

under the duvet

not ready to face the reality of the day

of this day

of any day

she's thinking of other lives

other loves

other chances

other hills

other weddings

other races

other garage forecourts after closing time

laughing as the rain beats down

in its own private joke

and that beautiful wistful unattainable what if

the alarm sounds again

loud

insistent

the unstinting unavoidable reminder of the life that is the here and
the now

the gap between her daydream and the reality we are only left to
imagine

ley-lines

the scars on my body that you see

they are not damage

they are ley-lines

mapping out the geography

of my history

you can wend your way around me on these marks

navigate the tales of my childhood

my transition into adulthood

the falls, the scrapes

the lumps removed

the bones realigned

each one a story of pain

poignant, beautiful

but never damage

these lines of silver define me

this is my topography

what makes me me

but the scars on the inside

oh my love, my lover

you have to be so much closer than that to see those

let the field grow back

take a year off

rest

let the field grow back

growing is not always about pushing, striving

sometimes it is about waiting until the conditions are right

letting the potential bide its time

just because something lies fallow does not mean it is dormant

the grass growing under your feet does not mean that one day
there won't be flowers

or potatoes

it really depends on your point of view

so rest

lay back your weary head and let the dark earth support you

you will grow back

the field will grow back

but

for now

take that year off

dad?

your shirts still hang in the wardrobe

with creases nicely pressed

your jumpers, neatly folded,

sit on a shelf, aligned by angles

shoes

pairs

two, thereof

one black, one brown

buffed and shining

plus that worn-out pair you were always going to throw out

but saved for dog walks and gardening days

ties strewn over a coat peg

old socks, once lovingly darned

underpants,

marks and spencer's, obviously

and handkerchiefs, carefully ironed

a man's attire,

a man's life

all contained in one wardrobe

a sartorial book for anyone to read

all that is missing is you

and also your passport

cat

you are in all my close places
you do not announce your visit
or tell me of your intentions
you arrive uninvited
and stay beyond your welcome

you are like a cat
as selfish
as indifferent
you come and go as you please
i no longer know if
you will be in my bed at night
or gone before the sunrise
your presence is as intangible
as morning mist
and infinitely less reliable

i can no longer live
with the uncertainty
the hope
the crush of disappointment
i have thrown away the food bowls
and boarded up my emotional cat-flap

the beat of her existence

when she arrives it's the favourite part of my day.
as she walks in and i see her for the first time
every part of me tightens

i try not to look closely as she strips off her coat.
i try not to listen to her talk with the others.
i fail, of course.
that flex of her shoulders,
the curve of her breast,
her voice,
her smile.
or its absence.
she wears her moods as other women wear clothes

the beat of her existence makes my workday worthwhile.

a ring flashes on her left hand.
and i say nothing.

real life

how i hate my consciously-awake moments

when dreaming of you is not an option

and real life strides past the fantasy

jolting me from my daydreams

my wishes

my imagined anticipations

when i have to remember that you are not here

on your knees

and your mouth isn't

there

and this isn't actually

happening

the jolt of reality is a kick to my subconscious

shocking me back to attention

and i have to remember

this isn't a safe place for me to visit anymore

yet we have so much more fun there

i really think you should come round sometime

summer can't last forever

it's time to stop touching the sun when your arms no longer reach.

let it go

let it dip below the horizon, beyond your gaze, out of your reach

that day is done, that summer is gone

and it will never be again

treasure those memories as the earth beds down for winter

there will be new days, new seasons

but no matter how golden, now matter how precious, this one is sinking, this day has set

it is time to let go.

time to say goodbye.

it's time to stop touching the sun when your arms no longer reach.

she stood amongst them

she stood amongst them

> her thoughts were as their thoughts

>> bold. patriotic. hopeful.

a new country. a brighter time. a better age.

death to the enemy. liberation. let fire and fury rain down on our oppressors, our opposers.

> the crowd cheered. whooped. chanted. sang.

>> and she made notes.

her thoughts were as their thoughts. but not to their anthem.

her heart swore allegiance elsewhere long ago. she beats to a different drum.

every cheer, every whoop, every note sung; all signposting a way to how this city could be taken, this civilisation fall.

> she stood amongst them

>> not with them

all kinds of trouble

the danger-signs were out the day we met.

the strong revolving beam of the lighthouse, guiding ships safe to harbour; while we stayed cloaked in the darkness and flung ourselves heedlessly onto the rocks.

please reduce your speed, flashed the boards on the motorway.

we hurtled straight past, foot to the floor, hungry for more.

the red warning flag at the beach for the swimmers

but in we plunged, soaking wet, desperate and regardless.

please drink responsibly, the label read. we didn't. we thirsted. and ordered more.

fragments of us are scattered violently everywhere; we should have read the signs

connections

eye contact, skin on skin contact.

to taste, to touch, to smell.

so many different ways to connect to a person, to know them, to understand them.

we can eat and drink and dance.

we can lie under the stars and hold hands until the sun rises.

we can talk of life and of love and of the world around us, how we see it, what it is, what it means.

our paths can cross in a myriad of ways and light up our worlds with contact.

and so

we lie in bed alone,

making random connections

on our phones.

ferocious tangle

he surveyed the mess unenthusiastically
he hadn't meant for things to get this bad
he only stopped paying attention for a little while
but now, this heap and tangle
this mess of loose endings
unfound beginnings

he stared, lost
perplexed
it was a knot of gordian proportions
he didn't now where to begin
which strand to pull on
which end to loose
how to know what would make it better
how to fix this ferocious tangle
he didn't want to get it wrong and make things worse
his fingers slipped and stumbled

until, eventually, his headphones were free once more

the end

"i loved you once," she said quietly

his hand moved to cover hers

"why did you never tell me?"

she considered the question, thinking of the late night messages, the phonecalls, the photos, the walks and talks shared together.

she remembered the tears he soaked her shoulder with, the silent way she held him, creating a safe space for the emotion to come out.

the steadfast nature of his presence, always meant to be there.

"i never stopped telling you" she replied

as all around them the machines whirred and beeped, the never-silent measurement of a life at its end

your hand

i saw you the moment i walked though the door

heard you

wanted you

your hand rested on the small of my back as we greeted each other

it was genial, pleasant, the merest air kiss skimming a cheek

the politest of social small talk

but i could feel the heat of you through my clothes

days later i am still amazed that there isn't a scorch mark on my skin

a perfectly outlined hand-print

like the ones children make for their mothers in nursery

with poster paints and lots of mess

on reflection, our relationship is not that dissimilar

words alone

words alone cannot conjure love

we edit our best selves into what is most pleasing,

mirroring desires with our prose

words cannot tell me the shape of your mouth

as you smile

or what questions

dance behind your eyes

words cannot convey the way your t-shirt rises

as you throw a ball for a dog

patiently walking by your side

beautiful speeches do not show

if you are tolerant of waiters who

mistake your order

or deliver wine that is

corked

before you protest yes, my lover, yes

i would urge you to read

the tale of cyrano de bergerac

lovers

we do not make eye contact

it is too intimate a setting for that

i am exquisitely aware of the shape of you

the smell of you

your proximity is making my head swim

but there are others too

daringly close

almost touching

their hot bodies wanting to be a part of our action

a shudder

a wrench

and we stop

then you are gone

the others too

the space around me seems too much

and i blink, disorientated

and the central line continues westward

as sweat traces its way down my spine with the emotional accuracy
of a lover

friday night

i decide to take a bath. slow, leisurely, glass of wine, music softly playing. some pampering, some self care.

post bath, i moisturise. i'm daydreaming about what to have for dinner. i apply my body lotion without even thinking about it.

perhaps there was too much wine in the glass. my hand slips and my fingernail rakes painfully across my nipple. in other circumstances i might enjoy it. but not that like this.

and that's why i'm naked and alone in my bedroom on a friday night,

half covered in body lotion and screaming 'fuck' for all the wrong reasons.

adoration

they adore you

you are the sole reason for their existence

no-one has ever paid them such intense devoted attention

you are wrapped in them and they are rapt in you

they feel the intensity of your gaze

as you struggle to take on every nuance of their being

to grasp their truth and any possible meaning

they yearn to hold you captivated

you are their raison d'être

your attention completes them

all they have ever wanted was to be on your lips

but did you know that when you finish the book

and close the cover

the words cry

the woods

the woods can be a strange place for walking

the air feels different here. the light too, casting dappled shade over the bluebell carpet.

the wind whips through the trees, making branches creak. the only other sounds are birds singing and the panting of tired dogs.

there's different paths to take, some carved out of the tramp of walkers feet, year upon year. some paths are less well-trodden, places less explored.

and then there's an elderly man walking towards you, smiling, carrying a plastic bag and a chainsaw.

like i said, the woods can be a strange place for walking

burning

i know you are there yet i can't look at you
the sight of you burn my eyes
every time i sense you so much emotion rises inside me
i fear i will be set alight

how can you not know?
how can you not feel it?

each time our paths
cross lava flows through
my veins,
i am heated
from my very core
flushed
with the fire consuming me
i keep my eyes,
my attention, averted
for this fear of burning you,
scalding you with this intensity

but perhaps i'm actually afraid that it wouldn't affect you at all

what to remember after the end of a relationship

and yet you will be ok.

a morning will come where it isn't the first thought that kicks you in the head on waking.

you'll catch a pretty girl checking you out.

the sun will shine.

you'll eat something wonderful and talk about it.

and you'll realise there is still a whole world to explore out there and you have a vital place in it.

that this would be less of a brilliant place if you weren't here.

time will pass and the violent see-saw of emotions will start to ease.

time doesn't heal, it just helps with our perspective.

a city at 2 in the morning

it's two in the morning

in a city filled with culture and drunk tourists

the sound of laughter rises as a group leave the club

their words cutting through the fog-filled air

there's some good natured shouting as one moves away

then the rising steam from a piss taken behind a bin

further down the street a girl leans on a wall

alone

too drunk to walk

too desperate to be home to stand still

and in a doorway a homeless man tries to sleep

in his makeshift house of crumpled cardboard and the discarded
remnants of an earlier life

how many times

do you have any idea

how many times a woman has pretended to laugh

in boredom

as your tedious explanations seared through her brain

or

how many times a woman has become voiceless

to hide her disgust

as your hands held her waist and moved between her thighs

or

how many times a woman has been motionless

in fear

as your lips and hands claimed her body and invaded her unwilling space

do you have any idea

how many times

these things have happened to you

do you have any idea

how to feel

to feel what this feels like

perfectly noticed

you had been perfectly noticed

that first night

every single inch of you admired, noted

recorded

the next morning was hard, saying goodbye

perhaps something had gone wrong

in the testing phase

but the memories remained

even though you did not

now your movements are on auto-play

and the soft sounds of your voice the soundtrack

to the video-loop in our laboratory

we never knew what it was that made you so intrinsically perfectly
you

but our scientists have been working on this for years

you had been perfectly noticed

that first night

and now you will be perfectly replicated

fierce motherhood

my hips curve

my breasts bloom

blood drips down my thighs

my heart beats

my hormones ebb

and swell

my love is fierce

and uncompromising

are you a creature of my womb

or of my imagination?

and yet does your voice count louder because a child fractured your cervix?

does that scar across your stomach as count more or less than my wounds?

a heartbeat on a scan never seen

a cry wheeled away across a private ward

how dare you, how dare you, tell me i cannot speak "as a mother"

how dare you tell me i cannot speak.

yearning

i pine to touch you.

to hold you in my hands.

to smell the scent of you, to let my fingers trace your outlines, for my ears to delight at your sounds, to let my mouth taste the shape of you.

it's been long, so long. too long.

i've imagined every angle of you, every twist and every turn, all in exquisite detail.

the anticipation.

i know when it happens you will not disappoint.

but your author has not written you yet. and so, next book in the series, i yearn for you as i would yearn for a lover.

loaf

i watched your fireworks through the gaps in the trees

the occasional darting arc of colour

the sulphuric smell drifting back to my half open window

                i wasn't allowed to hold a sparkler of my own

i could see your fire burning

the lick of flames on wood

sparks crackling into the night sky

            i wasn't permitted to go closer and enjoy the heat

to those who say it is better to have half a loaf than no loaf at all

i ask

how long has it been since every day you didn't have a fresh loaf of
your own?

acknowledgements

writing is very much a solo occupation but no writer is an island.

therefore, i would like to thank kate foster as without her inspiration these words would never have come to be.

thank you to cynefin road for being my second home, welcoming me, sheltering me, and believing in me.

thank you to everyone who ever shared a #100wordstory online, left me feedback, encouraged me to do more. this book would not have existed without your support.

and finally, thank you to my mum and dad who gave me a love of reading and words from the very start.

stephanie shields.

Cynefin
ROAD

i didn't know

i didn't know, in june 2015

that this would be a thing.

i didn't know that a simple nudge

a suggestion to do something new, something different

could change a mindset, change a world

i didn't know then

that i could create worlds and warnings

monsters and safe spaces

dangerous places

i didn't know it was possible

to tell a story with wit and brevity

to weave a fable, inspire a dream

i didn't know that one hundred words could be enough

or tell that much

but in august 2018 i do know

and now, so do you.

- thank you -